WEST SUFFOLK VILL/
From Elmswell to Elveden

A Portrait in Old Picture Postcards

by

David Osborne & Edward Wortley

S. B. Publications
1991

First published in 1991 by S.B. Publications,
Unit 2, The Old Station Yard, Pipe Gate, Nr. Market Drayton, Shropshire, TF9 4HY.

ISBN 1 870708 77 6

Typeset and printed by Geo. R. Reeve Ltd., Wymondham, Norfolk NR18 0BD.

CONTENTS

Front cover: The Street, Stanton, c. 1910

Abbreviations used: c – circa   p.u. – postally used.

ACKNOWLEDGEMENTS

The authors are indebted to the following people, without whom it would have been impossible to produce this book:

For the loan of various postcards,

Rhoda Bunn – pages 5, 11, 15, 20, 21, 23–25, 69–73, 75
Les Clarke – pages 31, 37
Dennis Cross – page 2
Huby Frost – pages 14, 16, 17
Basil Gowen – page 64
Sylvia Porter – pages 4, 10, 18, 19, 34

Additional research: Peter Nunn.

For permission to publish picture postcards published by them in the early years of this century,
W. Boughton & Son of Thetford
Pawsey of Bury St. Edmunds

For editing and proof-reading, Frank Rhodes and Susan Thompson of Stoke-on-Trent.

THE PICTURE POSTCARD

The first pictures on postcards in this country were published in 1894. These early picture cards were known as 'court cards', smaller in size than the standard cards of today, and sharing the space of one side with the correspondence. In 1902, the standard size was introduced and new Post Office regulations permitted one side of the postcard to be used for the illustration, and the reverse side for the correspondence and address.

During the early years of this century, millions of postcards were posted annually, encouraged by the cheap ½d postage rate and the vast output and choice of postcards published, depicting every subject imaginable. This era was known as the 'Golden Age of Postcards'.

Postcard collecting became a national craze and almost every household could boast of an album of cards for visitors to see and admire. The usage and collection of postcards remained very popular until the end of World War I, after which it went into a gradual decline, caused mainly by a rise in postage rates and the increased use of the telephone. Many fine collections were to lie dormant for many years and it is only during the last fifteen years that they have been rediscovered and today postcard collecting is as popular as ever.

Topographical cards are the most sought after by today's collectors. Suffolk cards are no exception and are in great demand, especially the better photographic examples of a collector's home town or village.

During the 'Golden Age' there were numerous postcard publishers, including Raphael Tuck, Valentines, Judges, W.H. Smith and Jarrolds, who started producing postcards in the late 1890s and are still publishing today. Local publishers included W. Boughton of Thetford, L. Pawsey of Bury St. Edmunds and F. Etheridge of Stanton, all combining to leave a comprehensive record of village life and the countryside.

P. STANDLEY
Founder member of Norfolk Postcard Club.

INTRODUCTION

Our journey, in this modest publication, takes us through most of the villages that form the north-east corner of West Suffolk, beginning at Elmswell and ending at Elveden; as the crow flies, a distance of 14 miles. The route that we follow, however, takes us for 65 miles or thereabouts, along the major and minor roads that traverse the ancient parish boundaries and well-cared-for countryside. It is a landscape as varied in its appearance as the villages that we visit. The word 'village' may mean different things to many people: a small community of neat cottages and houses, centred around a green and the parish church; a long straggling street of curious shops, houses and inns; a scattered collection of vernacular buildings, surrounded by arable and pasture land.

Whatever our concept may be, we can be sure to find an ancient parish church, once the religious and social centre of village life, and often the most substantial building to be found there. Amongst the cottages and other dwellings we can also expect to find a few large houses: a manor house or hall; the minister's house; and farm houses. Other buildings and features that often form the village landscape include chapels, public houses and community halls, barns and mills, stores and blacksmiths' shops, ponds, greens, commons and enclosed fields. All have been shaped and re-shaped by countless generations of villagers.

Since the early years of this century, when most of the postcards in this book were first published, the character and appearance of the village has inevitably changed. The village is less an isolated community, clothed in its customs and traditions, sustained by agriculture and a range of local crafts and services. Many villages are now dormitory settlements, extensions of nearby large towns, which provide employment opportunities, with shopping and leisure facilities only a few minutes motor journey away. Nevertheless, with a few exceptions, villages are still as popular a place to live as they have ever been, particularly for retired people.

We hope that the picture postcards selected in this portrait of West Suffolk villages, reflecting something of the past, will appeal particularly to those who have a connection with, and love of, the places that we have featured.

David Osborne and Edward Wortley
1991

ELMSWELL CHURCH.

THE CHURCH OF ST. JOHN THE DIVINE, ELMSWELL, p.u. 1920

The church stands on the side of a hill at the western edge of the village. Viewed from the west it can be seen from a considerable distance. It is said that Benedictine monks from the Abbey of Bury St. Edmunds built Elmswell's parish church. The handsome fifteenth-century tower was thoroughly restored in 1980–81, and on a clear day, from its lofty battlements, it is possible to see the spire of St. John's Church at Bury St. Edmunds, eight miles away. Elmswell has grown from a small, agricultural community of 451 people in 1801, into a large village of 2,127 inhabitants (1981 census). Situated in the so-called 'A45 corridor', Elmswell's population continues to grow.

ELMSWELL.

THE RAILWAY STATION, ELMSWELL, p.u. 1916

Elmswell's railway station was probably built soon after the opening of the railway line between Ipswich and Bury St. Edmunds in December 1846. The line was extended from Bury St. Edmunds to Newmarket in 1854. In its heyday, Elmswell had a station master, two porters, three signalmen and a clerk. Perhaps its busiest time was during the 1939–45 war, when tons of munitions, as well as personnel, were handled for the nearby airfield at Great Ashfield. Since the early 1960s, Elmswell station has gradually declined. In 1964 the local sidings were closed to goods traffic, and with the introduction of pay trains in 1967, the station became an unmanned halt. The main buildings were demolished in 1974 and finally, in 1986, the old signal-box was dismantled.

STATION ROAD, ELMSWELL, p.u. 1918

In the foreground is the tailor shop premises of Herbert Aldridge, now a hairdressing salon. Adjacent stands The Old Bank House, a fine, timber-framed and jettied building, recently refurbished after standing empty and dilapidated for many years. Next door is an early-twentieth-century house. Beyond is the signboard of the Lion Inn, once the Red Lion, and before that the Swan. The Lion closed its doors in 1934 and is now a private residence called The Beeches.

3

THE BACON FACTORY, ELMSWELL, c. 1920

In 1910 a group of Suffolk pig farmers formed a co-operative to process their own pigs for the bacon and pork markets. The following year they had this factory built at Elmswell, on land just off the Ashfield Road. Then known as the St. Edmundsbury & Ipswich Bacon Factory Ltd, it processed about 230 pigs each week and employed only a small number of people. Now the old factory buildings have gone and a large, modern factory occupies the site, producing a wide variety of British bacon and pork products.

T.F. HICKS, BAKER OF ELMSWELL, c. 1915

This superb study of a baker's boy on his rounds, is by an anonymous postcard publisher. Thomas Hicks, baker and confectioner, is recorded as trading at Elmswell from c. 1904–1922. It was once a common sight to see local traders and itinerant tradesmen carrying their wares about the countryside on foot, bicycle or horse and cart. These included bakers, butchers, fishmongers, game and general dealers.

THE SCHOOL, NORTON, p.u. 1910

Norton school, in the right foreground, was built in 1836 as a National School for 150 children. The National Society for the Education of the Poor in the Principles of the Established Church was formed in 1811 by Andrew Bell (1753–1832). By 1851 the Society controlled over 17,000 schools. Norton's National School later became a Public Elementary School. The old school was closed in 1965 and sold in 1968. It is now almost unrecognisable since becoming a private residence called 'Ponderoasa'. A new village school, now called Norton Voluntary Controlled First School, was opened in 1965.

THE HORSESHOES INN, NORTON, p.u. 1922

The thatched-roofed Horseshoes stood on the outskirts of the village, on the road to Great Ashfield. It was badly damaged by fire in 1971 and soon afterwards demolished. The site is now empty. The message on the reverse of this postcard is interesting. It was sent by a woman living at Norton's Salvation Army Headquarters: 'It is our Junior Anniversary on Sunday, and the children doing a meeting Wednesday evening. I am in my glory, teaching them drills, dialogues, etc. . . . I have an open-air at a village 9 miles away Tuesday evening. How would that suit you, cycle 9 miles, two open-airs and then cycle 9 miles home . . . .'

L., P. & Co.   THE HALL, STOWLANGTOFT, SUFFOLK.   447

THE HALL, STOWLANGTOFT, p.u. 1904

This is one of many picture postcards published in the early years of this century by L. Pawsey & Co. of Bury St. Edmunds. Stowlangtoft Hall was built in 1859 for Henry Wilson, J.P., Lord of the Manor or Stowlangtoft. It replaced an earlier Manor House, known as Stow Hall, that stood on the opposite bank of the River Blackbourne. Many of the 'greater country houses' are sited on, or near to, the site of a medieval manor house. The Prince of Wales, later King Edward VII, occasionally visited Stowlangtoft Hall, when shooting game on the estate. Since the mid-1960s Stowlangtoft Hall has been a private residential home for the elderly.

THE CHURCH, HUNSTON, SUFFOLK. 459

ST. MICHAEL'S CHURCH, HUNSTON, c. 1905

This small but interesting church stands secluded at the end of a rough track, next to farm buildings and a pond. Its origins are thought to be Norman. A relic of this period, a small piece of an ornamental arch, can be seen in an unusual place, at ground level by the north-east buttress of the chancel. Out of proportion to the smallness of the nave and chancel is a south transept, as can be seen from this view. The Registers of Baptisms, Marriages and Burials of the sparsely populated parish of Hunston date as far back as the middle of the sixteenth century. The population was 111 in 1911, and 38 households provided a population of 116 in 1981.

9

J & S 8315   PART OF VILLAGE, BADWELL ASH.

BADWELL ASH, c. 1910

A view looking along the main street, towards the village of Walsham-le-Willows. On the right, opposite the church of St. Mary, is the village shop and post office, known for many years as the Norwich Ale Stores. A Suffolk directory of 1900 lists Harry W. Keen, grocer, draper, ironmonger and hop merchant, post office. Mr. Keen, like many of his contemporaries, provided a wide range of goods and services. The Norwich Ale Store closed in 1987 and is now a private residence called Norwich House.

L., P. & Co.   HIGH STREET, WALSHAM-LE-WILLOWS, SUFFOLK.   258

THE STREET, WALSHAM-LE-WILLOWS, p.u. 1906

A view looking east along the attractive mixture of commercial and residential properties that form The Street. On the left is the Six Bells public house, a name no doubt associated with the six bells that hang in the belfry of St. Mary's Church, which stands opposite. Adjacent to the Six Bells is a row of nineteenth-century cottages. Beyond, is a large, white-coloured building that was once a medieval guildhall. It later became the parish workhouse, and is now divided into several dwellings. An old fire insurance company plate, or 'fire-mark', can still be seen fixed to the building.

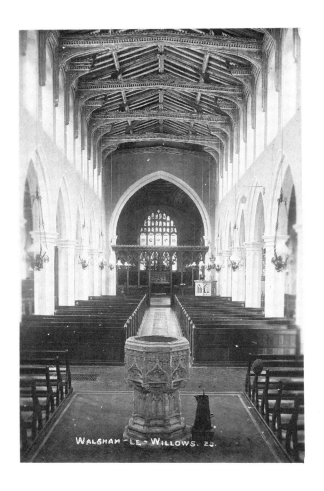

WALSHAM-LE-WILLOWS. 23.

ST. MARY'S CHURCH, WALSHAM-LE-WILLOWS, c. 1915

St. Mary's is a fine example of perpendicular architecture and is well worth a visit. In the foreground of this view is the intricately carved fourteenth-century font. Beyond is the spacious aisled nave, lighted from the clerestory windows above. Crowning it all is the superb single, hammer-beam roof of fifteenth-century timber work, said to be one of the finest examples in Suffolk. The nave is divided from the chancel by another fine example of fifteenth-century craftsmanship: a decorative rood screen, the rood having been removed, presumably in the sixteenth century. At the far end is the east window containing fragments of medieval glass, discovered in an old box and wrapped in an early-nineteenth-century newspaper. Below, is a late-nineteenth-century screen or reredos, depicting The Last Supper. The church registers of Baptisms, Marriages and Burials date from 1655, and are now kept in the West Suffolk Record Office, Bury St. Edmunds. They were once stored in the medieval parish chest, that can still be seen inside the church.

MILLERS ARCH, WALSHAM-LE-WILLOWS, c. 1910

Millers Arch is the name given to the small, arched brick bridge that spans the narrow stream beside the road. The pantiled roof of the building in the foreground is the former Swan public house, now a private residence known as Cygnet House. The adjacent thatched cottages have since been demolished. The site is now part of a builders' merchant's yard.

THE TEMPERANCE FÊTE, WALSHAM-LE-WILLOWS, c. 1908

A highlight for many people in Walsham was the annual Whit Monday Band of Hope and Blue Ribbon Temperance Fête. The festivities began in the morning at Millers Arch, with the arrival of one of Mr. Peter Nunn's traction engines, decorated for the occasion, and pulling a train of wagons. Once loaded up with its human cargo of excited children and schoolteachers, the procession began its short journey round the village and surrounding countryside, before returning home in time for lunch. In the afternoon the festivities continued with amusements, sports and a tea. No doubt a necessary qualification to participate at this event was the taking of 'the pledge'.

TEMPERANCE BAND, WALSHAM-LE-WILLOWS, 1906

The placard in front of the Temperance Band is inscribed: 'Walsham-le-Willows Temperance Band organised October 1893.' The band was formed by Harry Nunn, who started off as bandmaster, hon. secretary and treasurer. The above photograph was taken on New Year's Day 1906 by Mr. Cousins of Bury St. Edmunds. The band is seated in front of the Temperance Hall, built on a piece of Harry Nunn's land and opened on the 28 July, 1902. The hall survived as the main meeting place of the village until the early 1950s, when the Victory Memorial Hall was opened. *Left to right:* Frank Nunn, double bass; Leonard Finch, piccolo; Arthur Landymore, bombardon; Arthur Death, tenor horn; Frank Moore, tenor horn; Harry Cocksedge, bass; John Finch, clarinet; Wilfred Nunn, trombone; Harry Nunn, Frank Sayers, cornet; Harry Finch, baritone; Harry Hubbard, cornet; Bill Smith, cornet; Herman Lord, baritone; Phillip Finch, side drum; Oscar Frost, bass drum. Harry Cocksedge was famed in that, on a band outing to Lavenham, he walked round the parapet of Lavenham Church tower.

THE PARISH COUNCIL FIRE BRIGADE, WALSHAM-LE-WILLOWS, c. 1912

This view of the Walsham brigade, with their Merryweather manual engine and other fire-fighting equipment, was taken outside the Temperance Hall; standing on the left is the officer-in-charge, Captain Jonathan Hunt. The firemen on the right are holding 'fire cromes', for removing thatch from burning roofs. The old fire-engine house is now The Village Stores. In the early years of this century, most parishes maintained some form of fire-fighting equipment, if only a crome and fire buckets kept in the parish church. It was only the more populous parishes that went to the expense of maintaining a uniformed fire brigade and an efficient engine. However, well-equipped private fire brigades also existed in some parishes, such as Elveden, maintained by the major landowner.

FOUR ASHES FARM, WALSHAM-LE-WILLOWS, c. 1940

Dina and Darby, two chestnut Suffolk Punches, stand beside Fred Hubbard, ploughman to Lewis Waspe at his mixed farm. After the arrival of the Normans, the ancestors of our draught-horses were first bred as war horses, to carry the weight of armour-clad knights. Gradually the heavy horses replaced the use of oxen in plough teams and continued as the main source of power on Suffolk's farms until the 1940s. They were used at Four Ashes Farm until 1960.

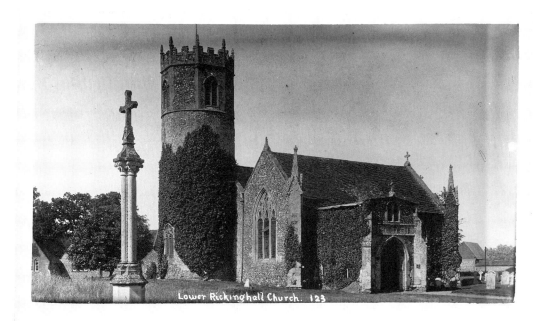

Lower Rickinghall Church. 123

ST. MARY'S CHURCH, RICKINGHALL INFERIOR, p.u. 1917

The picturesque, ivy-clad church stands beside the main road between Bury St. Edmunds and Diss, that passes through the village. One of its most attractive features is its circa twelfth-century round tower. The octagonal top was remodelled about 200 years later. The villages of Rickinghall Inferior and Rickinghall Superior, now known as the 'Rickinghalls', and the village of Botesdale merge into one settlement along the main road. At one time, the village of Rickinghall Superior was settled around its church (now redundant) south of the main road.

THE STREET, RICKINGHALL, c. 1905

A peaceful scene, now replaced by the noise of motor traffic. The bay-windowed shop front of Mr. A. Baldwin's drapery and grocery emporium has since been removed to reveal the original facade, and is once more a residential dwelling. Just beyond can be seen the signboard of the Golden Lion public house, now a private residence called Lion House. The Street straddles the parish boundary between Rickinghall Inferior (West Suffolk) and Superior (East Suffolk). East Suffolk County Council and West Suffolk County Council were replaced in 1974 by Suffolk County Council.

The Village, Hinderclay.   J 4455.   (Sutton's Series.)

THE VILLAGE, HINDERCLAY, c. 1915

A view taken at the village crossroads, looking towards Rickinghall, one and a half miles away. On the left can be seen the tower of St. Mary's Church. Following restoration work costing £750 in 1962, St. Mary's Church was rehallowed. The Village Sign now stands by the crossroads and modern houses line the road on the right, towards Rickinghall.

ST. MARGARET'S CHURCH, WATTISFIELD, p.u. 1906

Parishoners, perhaps in their 'Sunday best', present a tranquil scene as they pose for the photographer in front of the small parish church of St. Margaret. The church consists of a chancel, nave, north and south porches, and an embattled west tower. The site of St. Margaret's, like many of Suffolk's five hundred ancient churches, has probably been occupied by a building for Christian worship for at least 900 years. Wattisfield, spelt 'Watlesfelda' in the Domesday Book, had a population of 424 in 1911 and 427 in 1981.

THE SCHOOL, WATTISFIELD, c. 1905

'Watch the Birdie!' The photographer's camera captures the eighty-six pupils of Wattisfield's Primary School on this delightful postcard published by Jolly's Series, Wattisfield. The school was built in 1862 for 100 pupils, the cost being paid by the Rector and voluntary contributions from parishioners. According to Kelly's Directory of 1904, the school had an average attendance of 90 pupils; the population of the village was then about 408 (1901). By the late 1970s the number of pupils attending the school was down to about 20, and despite local protests, it was finally closed in 1986. Now, alas, the old school building stands empty and dilapidated.

9384

THE STREET HEPWORTH

THE STREET, HEPWORTH, c. 1930

Hepworth is a small village situated between Walsham-le-Willows and Barningham; population 416 (1911) and 400 (1971). This view, taken near the junction with Church Lane, has changed very little. The road at the Church Lane junction often became flooded after a rain fall, and was the subject of a great deal of correspondence and discussion by the Parish Council in their efforts to solve the problem. The road surface is now tarred and a proper pavement has been laid in front of the nearest cottages. Standing back from the road, on the left, and concealed from view, is the village 'pub': the 'Half Moon'.

CHURCH LANE, HEPWORTH, c. 1930

Although the parish church, dedicated to St. Peter, stands on high ground overlooking the village, it is concealed from view by the houses on the right of Church Lane. The church was virtually rebuilt in the early 1900s, after it was ravaged by fire on Easter Monday 1898. All that survived the fire was the tower, walls, porch and a few other pieces of the masonry. On the left is Church Farm. The thatched buildings there have since been replaced by more modern agricultural structures.

9764 Council Houses, Hepworth

COUNCIL HOUSES, HEPWORTH, c. 1930

These houses were erected by Brandon Rural District Council in the late 1920s on the outskirts of the village, on the road leading to Barningham. They were built to provide much-needed, good quality, rented homes for local 'working class' families. The water supply for these houses was obtained from a well, situated just behind the group of people seen in the picture. In the 1920s Hepworth had no mains water supply; it was 1952 before Hepworth received a piped water supply, and then only a temporary service from the nearby Shepherds Grove aerodrome.

STANTON CHAIR ROMAN VILLA. West Suffolk, 1936.

Hypocaust or Heating Vault of the Bath House. The Tiled Fireproof Floor of the Hot Bath was supported by the Pillars shown in the centre. On the right is the Furnace.

STANTON CHAIR ROMAN VILLA, c. 1936

The above is one of a set of two postcards published by Ipswich Corporation Museum Committee and sold at Stanton Chair Farm, the site of these excavations. The archaeologist in charge of the dig was the late Basil Brown, who went on to lead the team that first excavated the famous Saxon longship at Sutton Hoo.

ST. JOHN'S CHURCH, STANTON c. 1920

Although a petition was presented to unite the two parishes of St. John and All Saints, Stanton in 1590, they were finally consolidated in 1756. By the early years of the nineteenth-century St. John's Church was only used for burials, except for a time in 1875–76, when All Saints was restored, and again in 1906, when the tower of All Saints collapsed. The condition of St. John's was allowed to deteriorate; in 1962 the roof was removed and in 1974 it was put into the responsibility of the Redundant Churches Fund. The fourteenth-century tower, notable for its uncommon open archways to the north and south, contained four bells; one of them now hangs in the south bell turret of the cathedral in Bury St. Edmunds. Adjacent to the church is the old rectory, badly damaged by a fire in the 1930s. It has since been rebuilt, but not to the same design as its predecessor.

27

THE MILL, STANTON.

SMOCK MILL, STANTON, c. 1920

Stanton once had three windmills: Upthorpe post mill, now fully restored; a large post mill demolished during the Great War, apart from the two-storey roundhouse now converted into a private dwelling, and this smock mill, demolished in 1962. This is one of sixteen Vulcan series postcards depicting scenes of Stanton and published by F.W. Etheridge, grocer and draper, London House Stores, Stanton.

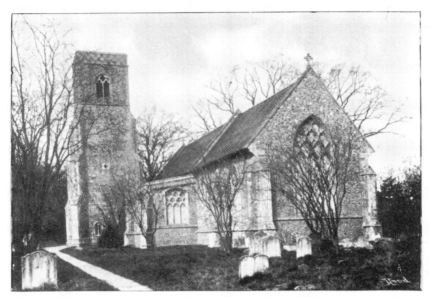

ALL SAINTS' CHURCH, STANTON, SUFFOLK. 133

ALL SAINTS CHURCH, STANTON, c. 1905

On the night of 5 March, 1906 the fourteenth-century south tower of All Saints collapsed. Fortunately it fell to the south, missing the nave and chancel. Alfred Shaw, the sexton, had a lucky escape that night. Only half an hour before the collapse he had rewound the tower clock. Although the clock was irrevocably damaged, the four bells in the tower survived unharmed. A temporary roof was placed over the surviving tower base until 1956, when it was replaced by the present bell chamber, at a cost of £1,700.

The Street, Stanton.

BRITANNIA SERIES. No. 661

THE STREET, STANTON, c. 1910

This is one of several Stanton postcard views published by W. Boughton & Son of Thetford. This view looks into The Street before the village War Memorial was erected at this road junction. A county directory for 1912 lists the following commercial businesses in the parish: 2 shopkeepers; 1 grocer, draper, patent medicine vendor, boot dealer and newsagent; 1 shopkeeper and photographer; 1 grocer and post office; 2 bakers; 1 butcher; 1 miller; 4 public houses; 2 beer retailers; 2 shoemakers; 1 saddler; 1 wheelwright; 1 builder; 1 bricklayer; 1 carpenter; 2 blacksmiths; 1 engineer and threshing machine proprietor; 1 agricultural engineer; 17 farmers.

ARMISTICE DAY, STANTON, 1921

Local school children surround the village War Memorial, unveiled just a few days earlier. Twenty-three men from the parish of Stanton gave their lives in the Great War; they were commemorated by the erection of this memorial, unveiled on 6 November, 1921. The memorial is inscribed: 'This monument is erected to the memory of the men of Stanton who made the supreme sacrifice in the Great War 1914–19'. A further four names were inscribed on the memorial after the 1939–45 war.

PLOUGHING ENGINES, STANTON, c. 1935

Sturgeon Brothers of Stanton were well known as agricultural engineers and contractors. They owned a number of steam-powered traction engines that were hired out, along with the necessary tackle and a team of operators, to local farmers and other contracting works. In this view can be seen a pair of 12h.p. ploughing engines, manufactured by John Fowler of Leeds. When ploughing, an engine was placed at opposite sides of the field and a steel wire rope, stored under each engine, was used to draw the plough backwards and forwards between them. The engine drivers communicated with each other by a series of short blasts on the engines' whistles.

HIGH STREET, IXWORTH, p.u. 1911

Since this photograph was taken over eighty years ago, major changes have occurred to some of the buildings in this view.Some of the buildings on the right were demolished to make way for Fordham's Garage and Ixworth fire station. (Both have since been moved to new sites). At the far end of the High Street, new housing development has taken place, destroying some of the trees.

THE WATER MILL, IXWORTH, c. 1910

This picturesque view of Ixworth Mill beside the river Blackbourne, is a typical rural scene from the early years of this century. In the foreground, a timber bridge carries the Ixworth to Thetford road. Ixworth Mill, once an important part of the local economy, continued to be used for milling until 1948. Now it is obsolete and derelict, a sad reminder of Suffolk's industrial past.

BIRD'S EYE VIEW, IXWORTH.
SUFFOLK.

L , P. & Co.   (345)   Photo, Randell

BIRD'S EYE VIEW, IXWORTH, c. 1906

Ixworth was once a small market town, centered along an important thoroughfare, now called the High Street. This view of the village, taken from the tower of St. Mary's Church, looks east across the High Street towards the fields in the background, now occupied by modern residential estates and enclosed by the Bypass Road opened in 1986.

THE CRYPT.

THE CRYPT, IXWORTH PRIORY, c. 1910

Ixworth Priory was founded in the 1170s as a house for Augustinian Canons. The priory was never large in numbers, not rising above seventeen. By the time the priory was dissolved, in 1537, it had acquired the whole of the Manor of Ixworth. In 1538 the ownership was granted to Richard Codrington and Elizabeth, his wife, in exchange for Nonesuch, in Surrey, where Henry VIII created his elaborate palace. A large, private residence called Ixworth Abbey now occupies much of the site, incorporating the well-preserved crypt or undercroft.

STOW LANE, IXWORTH, c. 1910

This view of Stow Lane, taken from the bottom of the High Street, shows the lime tree that stood there for many years. It was felled in 1971 after receiving several knocks from passing vehicles. The cottage standing behind the tree has also been demolished, increasing the width of the road at this once-busy road junction. On the right is a small, brick building where the village street water-cart was housed. In dry weather it was used to water the surface of the village roads and, hopefully, lay the dust. This end of Stow Lane is the site of the medieval market place, granted in 1384.

IXW 13   VIEW FROM THE BRIDGE, IXWORTH.

Copyright
P. U. Sergeant

VIEW FROM THE BRIDGE, IXWORTH, c. 1950

This is one of many picture postcards published by the famous national company of Francis Frith. This view looks south, across Ixworth Bridge, spanning the river Blackbourne, into the neighbouring parish of Pakenham. The boundary lies just beyond Bridge Farm house and adjoining cottages, standing on the right. In the distance is the Woolpack public house, situated in the parish of Pakenham and now a private residence.

Osier Peeling in Suffolk.　　　　　　　　　BRITANNIA SERIES.　　No. 459

OSIER PEELING IN SUFFOLK, p.u. 1906

Although the exact location of this view is unknown, it is nonetheless an interesting postcard, published by W. Boughton & Son of Thetford, and sent from someone living at the Manor Farm, Honington. It shows a number of uniformed boys, probably members of the Boys' Brigade, stripping the bark from white willow by the use of a 'brake' or willow stripper. In the foreground, stripped osiers are bundled ready for the skills of the osier-basket-maker. In the nineteenth-century basket- and sieve-makers could be found working in many of Suffolk's villages, but by the beginning of this century their craft was confined mainly to the towns.

THE STREET, PAKENHAM, p.u. 1935

The second building on the right is the former Telegraph public house, one of five pubs that once traded in the village, the others being the Woolpack, Royal Oak, Bell, and Fox. The only one that survives is the Fox. In the foreground is a small bridge that spans one of the many streams that flow into Pakenham Fen.

THE SCHOOL, PAKENHAM, c. 1935

Built in 1842 as a National School, this is one of two former schools that stand in the village today. Over the years it was considerably enlarged to provide places for the increasing numbers of children attending school, particularly after the 1870 Education Act, which provided a public elementary education for all children. The old school finally closed in 1967, replaced by a new school building. The new school closed just twenty-two years later, because of a decline in the number of children attending school there. On the left of the school can be seen a row of cottages, built in 1647, and once known as The Workhouse; since being restored in 1960 they are known as Church Green.

661   The Hall (south view), Great Barton, Suffolk.

THE HALL, GREAT BARTON, c. 1905

'Barton Hall Destroyed — A Great Midnight Blaze — Guests Watch Ravages of the Flames — Brigade Handicapped by Scarcity of Water — Valuable Paintings and Furniture Lost. Barton Hall, which has for centuries past been the pride of the parish of Great Barton . . . was totally destroyed in the early hours of Saturday morning . . . The glare of the fire could be seen for many miles . . . Thousands of spectators . . . The corner turrets stood up gaunt and bare; the magnificent conservatory was no more; the front wall had collapsed and inside were great heaps of red-hot masonry . . . The Hall was the property of Sir Henry C.J. Bunbury, Bart, a Justice of the Peace and a Deputy Lieutenant for Suffolk . . .' Extracts from the *Bury Free Press* 17 January 1914.

The Street, Great Barton, Suffolk. 380

THE STREET, GREAT BARTON, c. 1905

Villagers pose for the photographer in front of this attractive row of flint-and-brick-built cottages, owned by the Bunbury family of Great Barton Hall. The village post office and stores are at the far end of the row. A common feature of the 'closed' village or parish, in the possession of one major landowner, is the uniform appearance of the Estate cottages and houses, rented to the Estate employees. Built to the same design, they were usually of a much better quality than an agricultural labourer might find in the 'open' village.

MILL AND MILL HOUSE, GT. BARTON, SUFFOLK. 660

THE MILL, GREAT BARTON, c. 1905

The postmill with roundhouse at Great Barton, demolished about 1920, was one of about 180 windmills marked on a map of Suffolk surveyed between 1776–1783 by Joseph Hodkinson. One of the earliest documentary references to a windmill in England concerns that built at nearby Bury St. Edmunds towards the end of the twelfth-century. The decline of the windmill was brought about by the increased use of steam power and improved means of transporting flour and grain to large roller mills, often situated close to a port.

Bird's eye view from the church tower Fornham St Martin.

BIRD'S EYE VIEW FROM THE CHURCH TOWER, FORNHAM ST. MARTIN, c. 1910

This unusual view has changed considerably. It looks west, towards the once-navigable River Lark which flows across the middle landscape and forms part of the parish boundary. The cottages and old hall (now divided into three separate dwellings) still stand, but they are surrounded by new bungalows and houses, extending Old Hall Lane and creating Church Close. Some of the distant fields, in the neighbouring borough of Bury St. Edmunds, now contain a variety of buildings.

THE SAPPERS AT FORNHAM ST. MARTIN, c. 1916

Soldiers of the Royal Engineers parade in the main street, outside the Woolpack public house and the adjacent village post office. This is one of several postcards, photographed and published by W.R. Burrell of Fornham St. Martin, featuring troops stationed in the villages of West Suffolk during the Great War.

THE SCHOOL, FORNHAM ST. MARTIN, c. 1910

The camera is the focus of attention for these children standing outside the village school; the entrance porch of the school can be seen behind the children. As the school had no playground, it was probably a common sight to see them there. A school was first built here in 1836, and rebuilt in 1872 to conform to the 1870 Education Act. It was again enlarged in 1887 to accommodate up to 100 children. The School Log Books from 1870–1918 have survived. The following entry was written 15 September 1885: 'School re-opened after Harvest. Very low attendance, 43 at present. Holiday lengthened to six weeks, because the harvest was not finished.' The old school now serves as the Village Hall.

L, P & Co.　　　"CULFORD ARMS," INGHAM, SUFFOLK.　　　314

CULFORD ARMS, INGHAM, c. 1905

This public house remains a popular resort for locals and travellers along the main Bury – Thetford road. In the middle of the nineteenth-century it was known as the Griffin, but by the mid-1880s was known as the Culford Arms. A directory of 1912 lists: 'Harry Smith, brewer, maltster, farmer and coal merchant'; apparently, beer was still being brewed on the premises. Its present name is The Cadogan Arms. The Cadogan family owned the nearby Culford estate, which included part of the parish of Ingham, until it was sold in 1935.

L., P. & Co.   The Village, Ampton, Suffolk.   294

Never Absent.

Never Late.

THE VILLAGE, AMPTON, c. 1905

The above is a Sunday School Attendance Card, published as a postcard by L.P. Pawsey of Bury St. Edmunds, and given for good attendance, hence the proverb printed on the front. In the foreground of this view is the old Charity or Grammar School, founded in 1692 by James Calthorpe for the education of six poor boys from Ampton and the surrounding villages. Behind the school can be seen the top of the fifteenth-century church tower of St. Peter and St. Paul, restored by John Paley of Ampton Hall in 1889. The Hall, standing opposite the school, was burnt down in 1885 and rebuilt on the same site in 1892.

AMPTON: DOROTHY CALTHORPE ALMS-HOUSES.
(1693)
24 · IV · '37

ALMSHOUSES, AMPTON, c. 1937

In 1692 Dorothy Calthorpe of Ampton Hall left £1,000 for the building of these almshouses, for four poor women, on Ampton Green. Since then, part of the village Green has also been enclosed within the grounds of the Hall. Although the almshouses are still standing today, they are unoccupied, perhaps a reflection on the declining population of this village. In 1911 the population was 130; in 1981 it was just 33.

SKATING PARTY, LITTLE LIVERMERE, 1933

This party of skaters on Livermere Lake was photographed 29 January 1933, a period when it was not uncommon for the lake to freeze over. The lake is situated in Livermere Park, a parkland of 700 acres, much of which has since been ploughed up. Behind the skaters can be seen the tower of St. Peter's Church. Last used for regular worship in 1903, its roof was removed in 1954.

THE VILLAGE, TROSTON, SUFFOLK. 700

THE VILLAGE, TROSTON, c. 1905

A part of the village that has seen many changes to its appearance since this photograph was taken. Over the years all the cottages have been demolished, along with the small, circular thatched building, erected in 1808 by the Troston Poor's Estate as a coal house for the poor of the parish. These sites are now occupied by modern housing, although the old brick and flint garden walls survive, along with the former Wesleyan Methodist Chapel, built in 1891, and standing in the centre of this view. It is no longer a religious centre, but the village stores. The old village store and post office can be seen to the left of the chapel.

10,645 The Rectory, Honington.

THE RECTORY, HONINGTON, c. 1953

On the left is Honington Rectory, now known as Honington House. After the Church authorities sold this rectory, the minister for the parishes of Honington and Sapiston lived at Sapiston Rectory until the mid-1960s, when a new rectory was built in Honington and the one at Sapiston was sold. Since this view was taken, each side of the road towards Ixworth has been developed with modern housing, including the old Rectory garden. Note the letters 'WSCC' on the top of the old direction signpost; these stood for West Suffolk County Council.

VILLAGE SCENE, HONINGTON, c. 1915

The cottage on the right is the birthplace of the famous Suffolk poet Robert Bloomfield, born 3 December 1766. His poems, such as *The Fakenham Ghost, Barnham Water* and his most famous *The Farmer's Boy* are still appreciated and widely read. Included among Bloomfield's patrons was the Duke of Grafton of Euston Hall. Robert's father, George Bloomfield, died of smallpox, when Robert was a year old, and was buried in the churchyard of All Saints Church, opposite their home. Robert Bloomfield died in 1823 at Shefford, Bedfordshire.

PUMP GREEN, FAKENHAM MAGNA, p.u. 1906

Although all the buildings in this view still survive, it is a very different scene today. The blacksmith's shop, on the left, was converted into a double garage in 1975, at the same time as the adjacent Pump Green Cottages were converted into a single dwelling. Both of these buildings are now hidden from view by a tall screen of conifers. The two cottages on the right are now converted into a single dwelling, its thatched roof replaced by pantiles. In the foreground is the village pump, demolished by a passing motor vehicle some years ago. The Green is now given some protection from passing traffic by kerb stones, laid around its perimeter.

THE BEERHOUSE, FAKENHAM MAGNA, c. 1910

This view of the village beerhouse, the thatched building just beyond the bridge, was taken about five years before it was destroyed by a fire, never to be rebuilt. From the message on the reverse of this postcard, the people in this scene were either participating in, or spectating at an otter hunt along the banks of the River Blackbourne, that flows under the narrow bridge.

JUBILEE COTTAGES, FAKENHAM MAGNA, c. 1915

In 1887 Queen Victoria celebrated her Golden Jubilee, and to commemorate this great event, two identical groups of cottages, each containing three dwellings, were built in Barnham and Fakenham Magna by the Duke of Grafton for his Euston Estate. In the above view can be seen the entrance porch of the middle dwelling, which also contained the village reading room, a popular place for meetings and entertainment until it closed at the outbreak of the 1939–45 War. On the left of the main road can be seen outbuildings and the garden wall of Hall Farm.

RECTORY COTTAGE, FAKENHAM MAGNA, c. 1910

When the Rev. Redmond Bewley Caton moved into the Rectory in 1887, he decided that his head gardener should live in the adjacent Rectory Cottage, seen on the right. In the early years of this century the head gardener was a Mr. Edwards, who is remembered for his gardening skills. The Rectory Cottage, built of knapped flints and 'Thetford Greys', a local brick, became derelict in the 1970s, but has recently been restored by its new owner.

BORLEY'S HOUSE, SAPISTON, 1914

The burnt-out shell of Clement Borley's house is all that remains, after being struck by lightning and catching fire during a storm in October 1914. The owner of the property, the seventh Duke of Grafton, found temporary accommodation for his tenant and family at Chalk Farm, Fakenham Magna, a stop-gap tenure that was to last seventy years. After Clement Borley's death at Chalk Farm in January 1961, aged 100 years, his son Gerald continued there until 1984.

SAPISTON FROM BARDWELL ROAD. J 7669. (Kerley Series.)

BARDWELL ROAD, SAPISTON, c. 1935

This view of Sapiston has changed completely. The thatched cottage on the right has been replaced by an estate of local authority bungalows, built in the 1960s. The tiled cottage in the background still stands, while the trees on the opposite side of the road have disappeared to make way for another residential estate, erected in the late 1970s.

THE MILL, BARDWELL, c. 1930

Bardwell tower mill, built in the early 1820s, ceased working as a wind-powered mill in 1925, but continued in use for a few more years, powered by a motor. The mill was in a decayed condition by 1970, but after work carried out in the 1980s, it is now one of several Suffolk mills preserved and in working order.

VILLAGE SCENE, BARDWELL, c. 1910

Soaring above this lifeless scene that has changed little in over eighty years, is the lofty eighty-seven-feet-high tower of the ancient parish church, dedicated to St. Peter and St. Paul. The west tower, badly damaged in 1883 after being struck by lightning, is again in need of restoration, at an estimated cost of £40,000. In the distance, beside the entrance to the churchyard, can be seen a tiny building, built of brick and flint, and once the property of the Church. It came to be known as Bell Cottage; miniature bells carved out of wood decorate the façade of the now empty cottage. In the foreground, standing in Church Lane, is a former village store and post office, now part of a private dwelling. The road leading to the right is now called Quakers Lane, a reminder of the Society of Friends who built a Meeting House in the lane. By the middle of the nineteenth century the property was being used by the Methodists, who rebuilt it in the 1890s. It is now a private residence.

THE "GREEN MAN" INN, BARDWELL, SUFFOLK

GREEN MAN, BARDWELL, c. 1905

In the early years of this century, almost every village boasted of at least one public house. The 'pub' not only provided refreshments, but entertainment and a meeting place for local society. All sorts of business meetings were also held in the village inn: agricultural society meetings, benefit society meetings, coroners' inquests, manor courts and others besides. Bardwell's Green Man closed in 1966 but the village has two surviving public houses today, The Dun Cow and the Six Bells.

THE MILL, BARNINGHAM, c. 1915

Originally a maltings, a steam-powered mill was added in 1826. Steam continued to power the mill until 1931, when the engine was sold and moved to the Henry Ford Museum, Dearborn, Michigan, U.S.A. The Fison family, who were the original owners of the mill, had extensive business interests in Norfolk and Suffolk, as coal merchants, maltsters, millers, artificial manure and chemical manufacturers. In 1870 Barningham Mill was purchased by Mr. Walter Lingwood, who sold it in 1948 to the late Mr. Claude Aldridge, whose family continue to operate the mill.

L., P. & Co.   THE SCHOOL, BARNINGHAM, SUFFOLK.   208

THE SCHOOL, BARNINGHAM, c. 1905

The village school was opened in 1859 and now serves as a First School. In this view, the children stand patiently to attention for the photographer, Mr. Hood. This is one of several views he took of Barningham that day, all published on picture postcards. In 1905 about sixty children attended the school, the same number as today.

THE BEECHES, CHURCH, AND CHURCH COTTAGE, BARNINGHAM, c. 1905

In 1872 Mr. Walter Lingwood rented the Beeches from Thomas Fison, and in 1892 finally purchased the property. Church Cottage was also owned by Mr. Lingwood. Today the Lingwood family still owns these properties; Mr. & Mrs. Michael Lingwood live in Church Cottage, while their son John and his family reside at the Beeches. Standing between the two properties can be seen St. Andrew's Church; its tower and nave built about 1440 and the chancel at least a century earlier.

VILLAGE SCENE, BARNINGHAM, c. 1915

Barningham's population of 412, in the year 1911, has increased over the years. The first local authority housing in the village was erected in the early 1930s, and development has continued with private housing over the last forty years. In the above view, the two thatched properties on the right still stand, the second one being Church Cottage. The buildings at the far end of the road have all been demolished, replaced in the early 1960s by Bishops Croft housing estate.

67

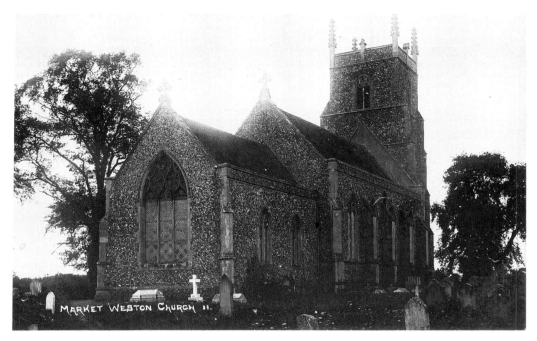

ST. MARY'S CHURCH, MARKET WESTON, c. 1920

St. Mary's is pleasantly situated, surrounded by fields and a fine view of the countryside. The fourteenth-century, square, decorated tower contains five bells, which were rung to announce all sorts of events and occasions, besides providing musical entertainment from the bell-ringers. In the nineteenth-century St. Mary's Church was restored: in 1846–47 over £3,000 was spent on refurbishment, including the rebuilding of the chancel, and in 1889 the chancel roof was raised, and a new vestry and belfry built. For centuries, parishioners have striven to maintain the fabric of their parish church. Over the course of time it has been continuously altered, repaired and re-shaped, sometimes because of a change in religious doctrine.

Greyhound Road, Hopton. (*Fiske's Series.*) J 1753.

GREYHOUND ROAD, HOPTON, c. 1910

Greyhound Road is now called Bury Road. On the left is the Greyhound Inn, once known as the Cherry Tree, now a private residence. Earlier this century there were four pubs in the village: the Chequers, Commercial, Greyhound and Vine; only the Vine survives. The meadow opposite the Greyhound was used for many years as a fairground, and the single-storey building beyond is an old blacksmith's shop. In the distance is the tower of All Saints Church.

ALL SAINTS CHURCH, HOPTON, c. 1930

The main fabric of All Saints Church, built of brick, flint and stone, dates from the fourteenth century. It consists of a chancel, nave and aisles, south porch and an embattled west tower. The remains of a spire that once adorned the tower, form the coping on the churchyard wall. The upper part of the tower was built in the eighteenth century, presumably as a result of the collapse or removal of the spire. Five of the six bells hanging in the tower were cast between 1629 and 1636 by John Draper of Thetford. The sixth, the treble bell, was cast at the Downham Market foundry of William Dobson in 1807. The clock was set in the tower in 1890 and in the early 1970s extensive repairs were made to the tower and nave roof.

SHOP CORNER, HOPTON, c. 1940

Standing against the village crossroads is the thatched Norfolk House, the old-established premises of Samuel H. Fiske &
Son, grocers, drapers, wine and spirit merchants and hardware dealers. Forty-six years ago the shop and adjacent premises
were destroyed by fire. A few years later a new brick-built shop, with adjoining house, was erected on the site and now
serves as the village store and post office. Note the kerbstones painted white, as a guide to pedestrians and vehicle drivers
during the war-time 'blackouts'.

Thurlow's Corner & Street, Hopton. *(Fiske's Series.)* J 1759.

THURLOW'S CORNER AND STREET, HOPTON, p.u. 1919

A view looking northwards, along High Street, towards the nearby Norfolk village of Garboldisham. On the left is the thatched High Gables, formerly Fern Villa, a private residence. Beyond can be seen the signboard of the Vine public house. Hopton, situated thirteen miles north-east of Bury St. Edmunds, had a population of 506 in 1911 and 524 in 1981.

THE STREET, HOPTON, p.u. 1923

A vehicle from a passing era and one from a new era stand outside the emporium of John W. Turnbull. Next door is Frederick Potter's butcher's shop. Clara Shickle (1885–1976), writing in the late 1950s, recalls: 'Sixty years ago this village was full of industry. We had three large provision shops which sold drapery as well. The people from the villages all round came here to do their weekly shopping. Anything special they wanted, it would mean a trip to Bury St. Edmunds in a carrier's cart or van, starting at eight in the morning; a three to three and a half hours journey.'

CHARLES GOODMAN, CARRIER OF HOPTON, c. 1910

Charles Goodman traded as a carrier from 1898 to 1923. He is still remembered by old residents of Hopton as a prompt and first-class carrier, who also hired out a wagonette, complete with groom and a pair of smartly turned-out horses. Every Friday he ran a regular service to Thetford, and on Wednesdays and Saturdays to Bury St. Edmunds for the market. In 1923 Mr. Goodman's business was taken over by H.F. Griffin, only to be bought out a short time later by C.E. Petch, who expanded as motor coach proprietors and now operate coach tours all over the United Kingdom and Europe. Note the old pram in this view, taken outside Goodman's premises in The Street.

FEN STREET, HOPTON, p.u. 1906

A view looking towards Knettishall that has changed very little. This road junction, where the signpost points the way to the nearby village of Coney Weston, is known locally as 'Fen Corner'. Fen Street is a small hamlet, half a mile west of the main village. This part of the parish is low-lying fenland, drained by a small stream that flows through Weston Fen, towards Hopton Fen and the Little Ouse river.

BLACKSMITH'S SHOP, CONEY WESTON, c. 1905

In the early years of this century, the blacksmith's shop was a common sight in most villages. It was here that farmers and others had their horses shod, farm implements and machinery repaired, and new items of ironware produced. In the above view a horse-drawn hay-rake can be seen outside the long-demolished 'smithy' at Coney Weston; the site is now occupied by a modern residential dwelling.

THE FIRST MONMOUTHS, CONEY WESTON, p.u. 1914

The 1st Monmouthshire Territorial Regiment is seen marching through Coney Weston in December 1914. The troops were billeted there and in the surrounding villages from 11 December 1914 until 10 January 1915 while they were engaged on training duties. The above view was photographed by Mr. Arthur Gregory Bloomfield, who kept the village post office and stores.

1st. Monmouths. Coney Weston.

THE HALL, CONEY WESTON, p.u. 1915

The south wing of this seventeenth-century mansion, enlarged in 1891, is believed to be the oldest part. This is one of a series of postcards of the Hall when it was owned by Harold Arthur Oliverson, who resided there 1903–1918. Like many other large country houses, it has undergone numerous changes to its appearance and uses. Since the early 1980s Coney Weston Hall has been a hotel and restaurant.

EUSTON HALL FROM THE PARK, c. 1910

Sir Henry Bennet, later Viscount Thetford and Earl of Arlington, one time Secretary of State and father-in-law of the first Duke of Grafton, rebuilt Euston Hall in the 1660s. The Hall was remodelled in the mid-1750s by Matthew Brettingham and survived virtually unaltered until 1902, when it was almost destroyed by fire. Again it was soon rebuilt on the same plan as before. In 1952 it was decided to demolish most of the house, as its large size made it unmanageable. The north wing, on the right of the above view, which survived the fire, still stands today, together with a small section of the west wing. In the foreground can be seen The King Charles Gates, the main entrance to the west front of the house before it was demolished.

THE VILLAGE, EUSTON, c. 1910

Local children pose for the photographer in another of these peaceful village scenes. The main road from Thetford, at the bottom right, is now wider and carries heavy motor traffic through the village towards the A45 trunk road. The buildings on the left still stand, although the second one in view, containing three dwellings, was later damaged by fire and when rebuilt was converted into two dwellings, its thatched roof replaced by pantiles. On the extreme right is the village school, closed in 1952.

FÊTE IN EUSTON PARK, 1907

In 1907 a grand fête was held in Euston Park to raise funds for the Honington Church Restoration Appeal. The previous year Mr. W. Weir, chief architect of the Society for the Protection of Ancient Buildings, wrote a pamphlet giving details of the appeal. This fancy goods stall was organised by the ladies of Coney Weston; on the left is Mrs. Bessie Bloomfield and on the right, Miss Emma Bloomfield. The lady in the centre is unknown.

VILLAGE SCENE, BARNHAM, c. 1910

The Rectory garden on the right of this view, looking west towards Elveden, has been reduced in size with the building of a modern residence. The thatched post office can also be seen on the right; it is now a private residence. The garden beyond belonged to a cottage that was gutted by a fire in 1968. The two thatched cottages on the left still stand, and are now known as Walnut Tree Cottage.

PRIMITIVE METHODIST CHAPEL, BARNHAM, c. 1906

In January 1882 the Reverend George Edwards, Primitive Methodist minister of the Thetford Circuit, organised negotiations with the sixth Duke of Grafton, concerning the purchase of a piece of land to build a chapel in Barnham. This had come as a result of a petition signed by 132 local methodists. In May 1882 the sixth Duke of Grafton died and negotiations continued with his son, the seventh Duke. Eventually a piece of land in Station Road, Barnham was obtained for the erection of a chapel. The foundation stone was laid by Mr. W. Pechey, former Mayor of Thetford, on the 14 April 1884; the opening service took place 14 July that year. On Sunday 15 July 1984 the chapel celebrated its centenary with a special service. Sadly, because of dwindling congregations, the chapel was closed on Sunday the 10 July 1988.

QUOITS CLUB, BARNHAM, 1913

As this postcard was published by R.J. Bantock of Thetford, it was thought to have been Thetford's Abbey Quoits Club, but it is now known to be the Barnham team after winning the Denny Cup in 1913. *Back row, left to right:* George Clarke, John Catchpole, Arthur Howlett, George Steward, Fredrick Flack. *Front row, left to right:* William Rumsey Frederick Steward, C. Chinery. Note: Each man is wearing a Denny Cup winner's medal on his watch chain. Earlier this century Barnham had two other quoits clubs: Barnham Heart of Oak, and Barnham Japs. Although quoits is still a popular game in several West Suffolk villages, it is no longer played at Barnham.

ELVEDEN HALL, c. 1910

Several well-known families have owned Elveden Hall and the estate since Sir John Clarke in 1550. Among these are Admiral Viscount Keppel, 1768–86; 4th Earl of Albermarle, 1786–1813; William Newton, 1813–1862; Maharajah Duleep Singh, 1863–1894; from then to the present day, the Earls of Iveagh. The Maharajah and his successor, the 1st Earl of Iveagh, greatly rebuilt and enlarged the hall into one of the largest and most most finely-furnished mansions in the region. This view was taken after the alterations. The hall has been unoccupied since the end of the 1939–45 War, and in 1984 it lost most of its elaborate furnishings; auctioned on the premises they fetched over six million pounds.

Post Office & Estate Office, Elveden. BRITANNIA SERIES No. 782

POST OFFICE AND ESTATE OFFICE, ELVEDEN, p.u. 1905

In the early 1900s the 1st Earl of Iveagh built a number of good quality brick dwellings on his estate, a policy that continued until after the 1939–45 War. The attractive design of the buildings can be seen in the above view and is typical of the estate, an area covering about 23,000 acres. Since the beginning of the nineteenth century the Elveden Estate has been greatly improved, particularly in the time of the 1st Earl of Iveagh, when vast tracts of uncultivated heathland were turned into good agricultural land, proving that commercial farming could be carried out on the light, sandy soils of the Breckland.

The Church, Euston, Suffolk. 905

ST. ANDREW'S CHURCH, ELVEDEN, c. 1904

This postcard, erroneously described as Euston Church, also appeared in Horace R. Barker's *West Suffolk Illustrated,* published in 1907 before the error was noticed. The church was restored in 1869 by the Maharajah Duleep Singh of Elveden Hall; the thatched roof was replaced with slates and new benches were installed. Between 1904 and 1906 his successor at the hall, the 1st Earl of Iveagh, built a new nave and chancel, adjoining on the north side of the ancient church, in order to accommodate all his estate employees and their families at service time. This new extension was dedicated to St. Patrick, while the old church became St. Andrew's chapel.

ELVEDEN NEW TOWER

NEW TOWER, ST. ANDREW'S AND ST. PATRICK'S CHURCH, ELVEDEN, c. 1925

This beautiful bell-tower with adjoining cloister, constructed of knapped flints and finely decorated, was built in 1922 by the 1st Earl of Iveagh, as a memorial to his late wife. The cloister connects the new tower to the chancel of the ancient church. The architect employed was W.D. Caroe, who, in the early 1900s, had been employed in the construction of the new church.
(See page 87).

Local titles published in the series: "A Portrait in Old Picture Postcards"

Peterborough, Vols. 1, 2 & 3
The Soke of Peterborough
Wicken – a fen village
The villages of Old Cambridgeshire
Ted Mott's Cambridge

Huntingdonshire, Vols. 1 & 2

Hertfordshire, Vols. 1, 2 and 3

Enfield
From Highgate to Hornsey
The Parish of St. Mary, Islington

Norwich, Vols. 1, 2 & 3
Holt and District
Melton Constable and Briston
Great Yarmouth, Vol. 1
Norfolk Broads
West Norfolk
Norfolk's Railways, Vol. 1; G.E.R.
Norfolk's Railways, Vol. 2; M.&G.N.
From Swaffham to Fakenham

Thetford, Brandon & District
Diss & District
Beccles & Bungay
East Suffolk
Lowestoft, Vol. 1

General Titles: Boys of the Brigade, Vol. 1
Farming Times: A Chronicle of Farming
Constabulary Duties: A History of Policing
The Amewsing Book of Cats
The Magic of Multiples: Twins and Triplets

Other titles available and in preparation. For full details write (enclosing S.A.E.) to:
S.B. Publications, Unit 2, The Old Station Yard, Pipe Gate, Market Drayton, Shropshire, TF9 4HY.